Rapid Knowl

*The Science of Deep Learning and
Information Retention.
A Field Guide for Teachers, Parents, and
Autodidacts.*

By Gunnar Stevenson

A Special Thanks

Thank you so much for purchasing my book! I hope you will enjoy the learning journey we're about to embark on!

To show you my gratitude, I created a FREE downloadable booklet about the three main teaching theories. These theories are the pillar on which modern education lies, therefore they contain essential knowledge for aspiring teachers.

Visit www.gunstevenson.com to download your FREE "Essential Teaching Theories Booklet!

Table of Contents

Introduction

On the first day of my sophomore year of high school, my literature teacher, Mrs. Miske, bewitched me with the dance of death. I was one of those obnoxious, rebellious teenagers of the '70s who knew well that appreciating poems and anything of the sort was not cool. Thus, most of my student career I sat through my literature classes with crossed arms and a bored-but-cocky look on my face, pretending not to care what my teachers had to say. I awaited my new literature teacher with the same attitude.

When she stepped into the classroom, I knew she was different. She was tall and skinny, with her back slightly hunched, fingertips symmetrically aligned and her two index fingers pressed to her lips. As if she wanted to say something but used all of her composure to keep the information inside. She seriously strolled to her desk without saying a word. I sat in the second row so I could fully appreciate her looks. It was unique. She wore every possible color I, as a young man, could identify. She combined her infinitely loose top with similar trousers, high heel boots, cardigan, and scarf in a way one couldn't quite tell if she was an eccentric fashion designer, a bohemian, or simply lacking any sense of style. Her blonde hair was cut in a short bob, but it was so messy that I concluded it must've been intentional. For a few moments she scanned the classroom with her sharp and intelligent black eyes.

The tension was tangible in the classroom. No one had any clue what to expect from this woman. Her appearance suggested that she was one of those laid-back, easygoing teachers who would shower us with As and go to the pub with us in a year. But her posture and expression hollered "do not mess with me."

"I'm an artist teacher," she said finally. "We will do things differently from now on."

And then, like a magician, she pulled out a small cassette player from one of her endlessly loose robes. The next moment, a loud song filled the classroom. It was an eerie, almost devilishly playful melody, with a prancing solo violin and the orchestra following. The experience was so unexpected and odd that I forgot about playing the cool guy and just closed my eyes, surrendering to the music. When the song finished, Mrs. Miske started reciting a poem in a ghostly tone:

"Zig, zig, zig, Death in cadence,
Striking with his heel a tomb,
Death at midnight plays a dance-tune,

Zig, zig, zig, on his violin.
The winter wind blows and the night is dark;
Moans are heard in the linden-trees.
Through the gloom, white skeletons pass,
Running and leaping in their shrouds.

Zig, zig, zig, each one is frisking.
The bones of the dancers are heard to crack-
But hist! of a sudden they quit the round,
They push forward, they fly; the cock has
crowed."
- "Danse Macabre" (Dance of Death)
by Henri Cazalis

When she was done, as if leaving a state of trance, she finally looked at us. "What did you feel during the song and while I recited the verses?" she asked a girl in the third row. The girl was bashful. Not only because of the shock of her blood being spilled first by the new teacher but also because she didn't know how to answer the question. What did she *feel*? No one ever asked that question from any of us in school.

As an outside observer I watched myself open my mouth and utter these words, "I felt exhilarated and scarred at the same time. The song was dark and demonic but captivating and melodic at the same time. Based on the poem you recited, I think the song was following the verses' narrative and emotional makeup. The dead were having a party at night and then dawn broke and the fun was over."

I had no idea where all that information came from. I was so embarrassed. My cheeks got redder than the Communist Manifesto. Everybody was dumbfounded, except Mrs. Miske. She was ecstatic. "Yes! Yes! Yes!" she rejoiced. "What is your name? That is exactly what happened!" She explained that the poem was called "Danse Macabre" (Dance of Death) by Henri Cazalis. And the composer Camille Saint-Saëns turned it into music, establishing a new genre called symphonic poem. Mrs. Miske added that indulging our senses in more forms of art about a given topic helps us understand what that art meant to convey to us.

The next moment she fished out a sizable book from another secret fold in her attire. She told us to go to her desk. The book was a collection of paintings about the dance of death. We saw Bernt Notke's Totentanz from the 15th century, Vincent of Kastav, Johannes de Castua. After the audio priming, we'd look with interest and amazement at the frescoes and paintings illustrating how the dance of death unites us all. Even at the age of seventeen, we understood the underlying morbidity and collective acquitting joy of death. We're all in this together, it's coming, better enjoy life.

From that day on, I was burning with curiosity and appreciation for Mrs. Miske's classes. She was strict and caring, interesting and interested. All her classes were a magical mix of artistic pleasures and sometimes bland literature. We didn't study. We learned. And the teaching tactics Mrs. Miske used were exceptional for facilitating understanding, deepen learning, and aiding information retention.

Achieving success such as that as a teacher or a learner is not easy in any circumstance. Especially not the one in which we find ourselves now.

Danse Macabre, 2020-2021

There is an ongoing fear among parents, students, and teachers that the 2020–2021 school year has been a bust as far as learning is considered. Many students have been relegated to online schooling, even at the earliest of levels. It's difficult to put a solid thumb down on what any of us are learning. What is being retained? How many students are paying attention? Even when parents and learners are heavily invested, there can be frustrations and challenges that are difficult to overcome.

How many parents are at home, struggling to teach concepts they learned ages ago, needing support to give their children the best possible education? How many students struggle with the material they need to learn without having a Mrs. Miske by their side? In many ways, parents and even students have morphed into the teacher's role as they attempt to teach and self-teach principles and information they may not be familiar with or have mastered themselves. If they do manage to decipher what the material requires, it simply takes up too much time. How can one accelerate acquiring understanding and learning?

The current educational climate has also been difficult for teachers, both new and experienced. It is challenging to create an engaging and dynamic learning environment online, especially for younger audiences. Less experienced teachers may be in even bigger trouble as they have fewer classroom management skills to fall back on. They may be more technologically savvy, which is an advantage.

What happens in the virtual learning space is that many students log on, turn off their camera and microphone, and promptly mentally check out. They are not present with any of their senses, they are not engaged with the material. All they do is the bare minimum, log in. There were bare-minimum students back in the good old days of traditional classrooms, too. I was one of them. I just showed up, smug face on, without showing any interest. But I was present. I still heard what teachers talked about.

I still made mental notes about what interested me and learned about the topic at home. I still had the chance to get absolutely drawn into Mrs. Miske's peculiar world, which follows me forty-five years later. I am so concerned about students who won't get this chance. About teachers who won't be able to share all they have to give. And about parents who are in the depths of despair for their precious children, who will not get full exposure to the most wonderful aspects of learning.

I wrote this book to help students, teachers, and parents teach, learn, and find fulfillment. The practices presented in this book help teachers and parents deliver information and autodidacts to facilitate their self-teaching process. I will help you discover your teaching style and connect with your students' learning styles. I will give you problem-solving strategies and creative approaches to teaching and education to ensure you or your children reach your educational goals.

Chapter 1: Teaching Styles

One of my favorite movies about being an educator is *Stand and Deliver*. It is based on the teaching career of Jaime Escalante in the early 1980s at James A. Garfield High School in East Los Angeles. While the movie is a fictional retelling, the information regarding who Jamie Escalante was as a teacher and educator isn't. At that time, the school served mainly working-class Latino students. Shortly after Escalante began working there, the school's accreditation was threatened.[1] Instead of focusing his classes on students who performed poorly, Escalante offered Advanced Placement (AP) calculus instead.[1] He found students to take his classes by promising them a bright future. If he taught these students calculus, they would have a real chance to pursue careers in engineering, computers, and electronics. He had a captivating allure to his personality that made his students believe in him and his approach.[1]

Jaime Escalante didn't just succeed. His teaching methods were wildly successful, so much so that in 1982 he gained national media attention when eighteen of his students passed the AP calculus exam, and the Educational Testing Service (ETS) stated the scores were suspicious.[1] Fourteen of the eighteen were asked to retake the exam and twelve agreed to do so.[1] All of them did well enough on the second test to have the scores from the first test reinstated.[1] In the following years, Escalante's students continued to perform well on ETS's

AP calculus exams. Eventually, due to overcrowding, a lack of appropriate resources, politics, and jealousy, Escalante's math program at Garfield High School collapsed.[1]

One of the reasons Jaime Escalante was able to be so successful with the students he taught was his teaching style, which we will discuss in this chapter. It's important to realize that not every teaching style works with every student, and all of them have their pros and cons. You will be able to identify your own default teaching style, but also realize what secondary and tertiary styles you may need to adopt in particular situations or when working with specific students.

What Are Teaching Styles?

Teaching styles represent your educational value system. They are rooted in the pedagogical approach one has toward education. In Jaime Escalante's case, his approach was to improve the futures of the students he taught through education. Escalante was likely an essentialist, an educator who stressed fundamental and factual knowledge as well as intellectual and moral standards.[2] Knowing your own teaching style and where it comes from helps you improve how you teach and in turn improve the student-related outcomes of teaching. As an educator, your teaching style helps you develop an approach to education within the learning environment so students can grasp the material most effectively.

Most of us don't choose our teaching style consciously. We define it by experimenting with several different styles, our strengths and weaknesses, and how we maximize student engagement. Our default teaching styles will also generally be what we are most comfortable with. With experience and self-awareness we can choose to include a mix of intentionally applied teaching tactics of different styles as the need arises.

Autodidacts might raise a brow: "How does this apply to me?" Well, let me expand on that. Whenever you sit down to learn something, you are teaching yourself to learn. Therefore, you also have a teaching style. The best way to identify it is by listening to your inner dialogue and the actions this inner chatter prompt you to do. For example, are you hard on yourself when you learn? Do you tell yourself things such as "I will try to learn this. If I can't, I will get help/give up/research the topic more," or "I will not get up from here until I understand this," or "Let's see how I learned similar things in the past"? All of these thoughts reveal a teaching style. If you can't reach your learning goals at the phase you envision, you may need to tweak how you teach yourself.

The late Dr. Anthony Grasha, professor of psychology at the University of Cincinnati, created a model of five teaching styles: expert, formal authority, personal model, facilitator, and delegator. We will discuss these styles in more depth later in this chapter, along with the other teaching styles such as authoritarian, permissive, uninvolved, and authoritative.

How Teaching Styles Affect Learning

Harry and Rosemary Wong, authors of *The First Days of School: How to Be an Effective Teacher* and *The Classroom Management Book*, state teaching styles have three primary goals:

- to develop effective classroom management techniques;
- create positive expectations in the classroom;
- and achieve mastery of the knowledge taught during lessons.

Teaching styles should be focused on learning objectives and student engagement. It is impossible to continuously meet every student's needs in every single lesson. We need to take the lesson and circumstances of the material into consideration based on both the topic and environment.

If we manage a large class of 100 students for a Biology 101 course, what kind of teaching method will likely work best? Will we be able to divide the students into small groups and let them learn independently as we circle the room, answering questions? Probably not. Due to the sheer size of this class and the factual nature of biology, we are likely to use a lecture-based approach and present ourselves as the authority. Now, let's say these same 100 students divide into groups of twenty-five to attend a biology lab. Is lecture still the appropriate method of teaching? Of course not. This setting is more conducive to peer teams and independent learning. We are close at hand to serve as a resource when needed.

Our students should be the main focus of teaching styles. While we may have a teaching style we are most comfortable with, we should also be aware that style won't work in every setting. It is essential we consciously apply other teaching styles in appropriate learning environments. Discussion circles, debates, lectures, experimentation, independent practice, project-based learning, and many additional techniques all have a place and purpose.

Teaching and Classroom Management Styles

One of the most commonly used classroom management models was created by developmental psychologist Diana Baumrind in 1971. Baumrind's model consists of four classroom management styles:

-authoritarian,

-uninvolved,

-permissive,

-and authoritative.

The authoritarian teacher maintains tight control over their classroom while having little involvement with students. This teacher will be the one you remember as being incredibly strict when you think back to your school days. They always assigned seats, prohibiting you from sitting close to your friends. There was absolutely no talking in this class. If you broke the class rules, the punishment was harsh and swift, often resulting in sitting out time in recess, detention, or being sent to the principal. Usually, this teacher knows very little about his students' personal lives and will not be making a home visit.

The uninvolved teacher has little control in the classroom and little involvement with their students. This teacher doesn't invest much time and energy into their job. Decisions more or less "fly by the seat of their pants." In this classroom, the students run the show, and the teacher has done nothing to disabuse them of this notion. They are checked out from their job as an educator and is doing the bare minimum to get by daily. The uninvolved teacher isn't invested in whether or not their students succeed. They are more concerned with how they make it through their day than anything else.

The permissive educator is highly involved with their students but has poor control over the class. They care deeply about their students, but they become more of a friend and less of a teacher due to this high level of involvement. They can no longer be an authority figure for their students. They put in tremendous effort and care into their lessons. Still, the class is so unruly they can't teach effectively. The students behave in any manner they want, and the permissive teacher does little, if anything, to punish inappropriate behavior. This educator encourages freedom of expression and for students to be themselves but does not include any accountability lessons.

The authoritative teacher has both a high amount of control and involvement with their students. They have rules, and they stick to them in a manner that is both firm and fair. They believe in positive reinforcement and praises students when they have earned it. They also apply practical consequences to inappropriate behavior. This teacher cares about their students and wants them to be successful. They know about their lives outside of school, and they check up on them periodically and when needed. They set their expectations high, but they are also reasonable to the individual circumstances a student may be facing (poverty, lack of parental support, lack of access to materials). The authoritative educator teaches autonomy and independence, but also the accountability that accompanies those privileges. Mrs. Miske embodied this style excellently.

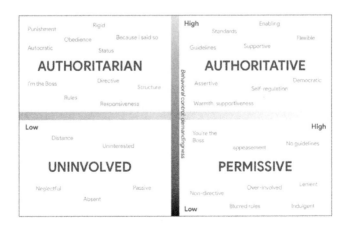

Picture 1: Diana Baumrind's Classroom Management Model[3]

These styles are based on the teacher's amount of control and engagement in the classroom. While we don't fit solidly in any one style, Baumrind's model does allow us, teachers, to assess our classroom management techniques and improve upon them when necessary.

When a classroom is not managed correctly, it is disruptive to everyone in the class. It takes away educational time. If we feel at a loss about handling difficult students, our life as a teacher can be particularly stressful. By understanding Baumrind's model, we can learn which situations call for which teaching styles and apply that method accordingly.

Ask yourself:

-Does this approach increase or decrease student engagement?

-Does it strengthen or weaken my control over the classroom?

The aim of good classroom management isn't to control students for the sake of control. It's to improve our effectiveness as educators and enhance the knowledge acquisition of our students.

When it comes to selecting what classroom management style to use and when, remember that students respond the best when they feel valued and have a voice. If, as authority figures, we choose to steamroll over them as if they don't matter, many students simply shut down. It is challenging to try and get them to open up again. It is tempting, especially if we have a difficult class, to tamp down on our students and maintain strict control to make teaching easier. But by doing so, students will lose respect for us and tune us out, choosing to ignore not only our rules but what we teach as well.

Try to grab elements from each part of Baumrind's model and apply them in various scenarios. When it comes to your students' health and safety, an authoritarian response is likely wholly appropriate. There can be no wiggle room there. However, in the days leading up to winter break, maybe you can be a little more permissive while also maintaining appropriate boundaries. Although the authoritative style sounds ideal, there may be a time when a student refuses to let you into their life, so you have to relax your expectations. All of these styles have pros and cons. Try and pull from each of them as the situation warrants.

Grasha's Teaching Styles

As previously mentioned, Anthony Grasha developed a model of five teaching styles in 1996:

-expert,

-formal authority,

-personal authority,

-facilitator,

-and delegator.

According to Grasha, all educators have some of these teaching styles in them, but they naturally lean toward one over the others.

Let's think about Grasha's teaching styles as a meal. A teacher's natural style would be the main dish, while the other styles would be looked at as the side dishes. Yet all of the styles are important as they collectively create and complete the full entree. Each part of the meal is meant to complement the others.

The expert style belongs to the teacher who focuses on high-level knowledge in a particular field to challenge students. Does this sound like anyone we've talked about before? Maybe Mr. Escalante used a bit of the expert teaching style when choosing to offer AP calculus to students at Garfield High School. The expert teacher's goal is to transfer as much information from their brain into the students' brains as possible. Unfortunately, we're human, and we haven't yet figured out how to plug ourselves into the cloud. Hence, the process is a bit more complicated. Those teachers who practice the expert teaching style aim to ensure their students are ready for the next test, quiz, or unit, thoroughly covering the subject backward, forward, and inside out.

The expert teaching style is often in large lecture halls and leans on slide decks or other multimedia presentations as tools. This educator is an authority figure retaining status by giving demonstrations and showing students what they are expected to know. This style is not well suited to teaching art courses where students are asked to create or perform. Nor is this style particularly good at taking the individual needs of each student into account.

The formal authority teaching style is usually cut and dry. When I was an assistant department head, I received a phone call from the director of disability services because she was having a hard time with one of the department's faculty, let's call him Tod, refusing to accommodate a visually impaired student with a test he could take. Tod wanted to display a picture of a part and have the students label the different components on their test sheets. How was that ever going to work if the student couldn't see the part being displayed? The Disability Services Office had gone through the standard protocol of requesting a test to meet the student's needs. Still, Tod was incensed that he was being asked to create a whole new test for one student.

After I hung up the phone, the director sent me a series of emails she'd exchanged with Tod. It was clear he considered himself the utmost authority on the subject matter being taught. He had every right to determine how students should be assessed. His guidelines and expectations for the course were set out in his syllabus and would not be deviated from. Despite repeated attempts, the director could not get Tod to understand he had a legal obligation to accommodate the student's disability despite his teaching style, which was deeply entrenched in formal authority.

While the example above is literally about a professor who was too rigid to understand when to make an exception, generally, the formal authority teaching style is very structured and follows that structure unwaveringly. This style is well suited to teaching in professions such as law or medicine because those subjects require specific sets of rules. Formal authority meets the needs of mature students, primarily those in a higher education setting. This type of educational style is also appropriate in super-size lecture halls of

250+ students, often used for introductory courses such as Chemistry 101 or Psychology 101. Due to this style's rigidity and the fact it relies heavily on memorization and little or no instructor interaction, it would not be appropriate in a K-12 academic setting.

As a reader of my book you can see that my main teaching style is the personal model. I often infuse my own experiences into my teaching approach. We're in the very first chapter of this book, and you know I have a nephew named Rob, my coolest teacher was Mrs. Miske, I like the movie *Stand and Deliver*, and I used to be an assistant department head with a bonehead faculty member. The personal model combines both the educator's personality and interests with the students' needs and the curriculum requirements.

In a classroom setting, this type of teacher is a guide to address questions and oversee work. Those who practice the personal authority teaching style rely more on encouraging students to follow directions and observe others if they need help with tasks. The personal authority educator focuses heavily on direct experience and watching students as they complete tasks.

This teaching often is not direct enough, which can be a problem. Without explicit instructions and answers to questions, some students simply cannot grasp the concepts and principles of the task at hand. When this happens, students are likely to become frustrated and feel like they are somehow lacking. This, of course, is not true. The teaching style and the learning style are simply not aligned.

This style works well in high-performing high school classes, such as AP, and higher education classes, as these students have usually mastered foundational concepts. One of the particular positives of the personal model is that it can be tailored to meet every student's needs in various subjects. One primary drawback to the personal model is trying to adapt the style to a hybrid course. This is a teaching style done best in person. There may be parts of this style you can adapt for fully online teaching, but hybrid courses would be a challenge.

Teachers who use the facilitator teaching style are warm and approachable; all the students love them. They inspire never-ending learning and curiosity. They are focused on students and the student-teacher relationship is of utmost importance. These young, moldable minds love to listen as this teacher educates them. They never scold them if they get an answer wrong, but instead asks a friend to help them get it right. As the students venture forward throughout the year, they've learned something, so the facilitator encourages them to deepen their knowledge.

The facilitator allows students to explore their education by making suggestions, then trying out those suggestions, and then coming back to the drawing board if those suggestions don't work. It is a teaching model that allows students to take a certain amount of control over their education and be responsible for their own learning. The role of the teacher is more to encourage and provide support when necessary. This teaching style is highly flexible and can meet the needs of students, but it can be extremely ineffective if the topic or student group requires a more structured approach. This style is ideal in graduate-level classes, particularly those with a research focus, as those students have enough discipline to be successful being left to their own devices.

Some of the facilitator's strengths are that it allows students to develop critical thinking skills as they ask questions, research, and find the answers to those questions. The facilitator style is both interactive and experiential and primarily learner-focused, so it can be the right fit for students with learning disabilities such as ADD or ADHD. These students would have a much harder time in learning environments with expert and formal authority teaching styles.

On the other hand, the facilitator style makes it harder to assess learning compared to other methods where one can test for knowledge. Assessment is still possible through evaluating skills and development. But it's difficult to tangibly measure and report these soft variables to the state board of education every year.

The delegator teaching style's main goal is to teach students to work independently and become self-reliant as they work in small peer groups. Although the teacher is present and available, their only function is that of a resource. This type of instructor doesn't give lectures or rely on other kinds of traditional teaching methods. Students who are adept and willing to put forth the effort to succeed in this type of learning environment can become independent learners with the autonomy to seek out knowledge on their own. However, students who lack the maturity and discipline it takes to guide their own learning and set their own educational goals are unlikely to succeed. Since the delegator teaching style doesn't rely on handholding, these students probably won't advance to a higher learning level.

Some of the delegator teaching style's positives are that it focuses more on inquiry-based learning and guided exploration. This allows the learner to take responsibility and have freedom of choice over their education, which is rarely found in a K-12 curriculum. Schools are often required to teach to a curriculum prescribed by their district or state. Some of the drawbacks include that the delegator teaching style removes the educator's authority. That can be a real problem in the classroom setting, where teachers need to maintain their authority for the health and safety of all their students. In this teaching style, the instructor has become more of a guide and much less of a formal educator.

Overall we can conclude that higher education instructors should have a different teaching style than those in the K-12 education system. As we have gone over previously, K-12 education relies more on authoritative teaching styles, which isn't always going to lead to the best outcomes in university settings. Students are actively involved in the teaching evaluation process for professors at the higher education level, but at the K-12 level, this rests solely in the realm of administrators.

In higher education settings, students find value in learning about their instructor's personal life or past experiences, as it makes both the professor easier to connect with and seem more human. In K-12 settings, teachers are strongly encouraged to maintain strict lines of division between their work and private lives as just the sheer look of impropriety can cost a teacher their job or even their license. Suppose students come to teachers with sensitive subjects such as concerns about expressing their sexuality or abuse in their homes. In that case, some teachers will pull in another teacher to help document the issue and provide a witness should any accusations occur later. In most states, the state board for educator certification exclusively controls teaching licenses. If a teacher's license is revoked, it can be impossible to have it reinstated.

As part of my preparation for writing this book, I went to do research in various school settings. I visited a community college that housed a rather popular mechatronics program that graduates many students equipped to go out in the industries in the area. The department head was a man who had over twenty years of industry experience. He said one of the challenges he faced when he first started the program was that many textbooks contained incorrect information to the extent that it could potentially kill a student who was working on currents and other electrical devices.

This department head had quite a reputation with the students he taught. He was known as extremely tough, and his students referred to him as "The Dark Lord." However, he took the time to develop a relationship with his students and stressed his reasons for being so severe. The Dark Lord deeply cared about the safety and success of his students. He was the first to arrive to school, personally supervising the safety equipment, tirelessly explaining and demonstrating safety procedures without ever getting frustrated. The students developed deep respect for this rigorous man and his courses and tried all the harder. The department head built this program from the ground up. He often relayed his own personal experience of not being able to afford to go to college after high school but having a family to support when he recruited students to his program. He talked to students about understanding a four-year college degree isn't for everyone, but having the skill to support yourself is something you cannot live without.

By sharing his personal struggles, he gave faith to his students. They knew what was possible to achieve. In higher education, course content isn't the only thing students are looking for. They want to see how the content will be useful after graduation. They are looking for dynamic, engaging, and personable educators.

Role models. As an assistant department head, I have read through many student evaluations of teaching, and they can be brutal. However, I've never gotten the impression this was done out of malice or vengeance. Students feel and know that the costs of higher education are high, and therefore they rightfully expect excellence in teaching.

You don't have to wait until the course is over to get feedback from your students. You can genuinely ask them what things you are doing well and what things you can improve upon. If you think people would be uncomfortable to share their honest opinion about you directly, you can set up an anonymous questionnaire on Typeform and send a link to them after classes. The anonymity should help the students provide constructive feedback without fear of retribution.

What's Your Teaching Style?

It's time to identify what teaching style you naturally default to, the pros and cons of that style, and when other styles might have more of an advantage over others. By giving you this information, you can evaluate if a specific style is best for the student population you are working with or the size of the class you are teaching. You'll be able to determine if your teaching style meets your students' needs and make the necessary adjustment if it doesn't. If you're not sure what your teaching style is, take this teaching style inventory: http://longleaf.net/teachingstyle.html.

What Is Active Learning?

Active learning is an approach contrasting the traditional teaching methods where students are the passive receivers of knowledge delivered by the educator. Here, students are encouraged to engage in the learning process. Active learning can be practiced in any field of study and can come in many forms. The most common ways to engage students in active learning is through group activities. Writing, talking, reflecting, or problem-solving interactive tasks are also great ways to enhance student participation in learning.

When it comes to using active learning techniques, Grasha's facilitator, delegator, and personal authority teaching styles are better suited to this goal than either the expert or formal authority styles. The aim is to have a balance between what students need to learn and how they learn it.

Even if you are in a situation where expert or formal authority are the most appropriate teaching styles, you can still incorporate active learning strategies. Active learning techniques help you become more approachable and contribute positively to building a strong relationship with the students you teach. Allow students to engage in feedback, give presentations, and conduct demonstrations.

Choose meaningful activities or questions. "When deciding what to ask or what to have students do, ask yourself:

- What are the most important things students should learn from this class session?

- What misconceptions or difficulties do students commonly have as it relates to this content?

- What kind of practice can students do that will help them prepare for an upcoming assignment or assessment?"[i]

Use the answers you gave to these questions to set up practices that enhance meaningful engagement and accelerated learning. Explain to your students the purpose of each activity. You don't need a lengthy explanation. Simply share the value students will get from giving their best shot at a task.

What is the Best Teaching Style for Modern Students?

Traditionally, teachers were encouraged not to combine teaching styles in an effort to become a teacher they were not. This advice seems to be the polar opposite of what is expected of modern teachers in a student-centered educational system. Our modern society requires teachers to use various styles for different types of students. Below are some things to take into consideration.

Instructors who rely on lectures as their primary teaching method are often referred to as the "sage on the stage." One of the main concepts used in these teaching styles is the empty vessel theory. The expert or formal authority assumes the minds of students are empty vessels waiting to be filled with knowledge, a hard drive waiting to receive downloads from the cloud. Critics of this theory argue that this type of teaching is outdated and needs to be modernized to reflect the educational values in 21st-century classrooms.

On the other hand, educators who favor more passive approaches like the expert and formal authority teaching styles argue that teaching styles such as the facilitator, delegator, and personal authority are heavily geared toward high achievers, such as gifted and talented students. This puts passive students, those who prefer to learn by observation and listening, at a disadvantage and further draws attention to the issue of teaching to meet the needs of every student.

There is a difference between knowledge and information. As teachers, we teach for mastery. Not for temporary retention of information that lasts long enough for a test to be taken and then promptly forgotten. We need to provide a solid foundation that more knowledge can be built upon. This is necessary so learners can understand more complicated and diverse concepts later. If students have cracks in their educational basics, they will crumble as the material they need to know becomes harder to understand.

The modern classroom is a technologically advanced one. Teachers who have managed to not keep up with technology have disadvantaged themselves and their students. Children as young as four years old who are entering pre-K are familiar with technology. They are using tablets like the Kindle Fire for kids and their parents' cellphones. It's not uncommon for young elementary-aged children to have their own cellphones, and nearly all students enter college with laptops. Many engineering and IT programs require students to have particular specifications on their laptops to use in their courses.

One of the best perks of technology in the classroom is the teachers' ability to assess their students' knowledge and progress over time. Programs like ClassFlow can help you measure student comprehension at the moment. Products such as iClickers can be interactive as they allow you to discover knowledge gaps in the classroom. The value of this type of in-the-moment assessment is being able to address issues immediately. It's faster than a formal assessment measure like a test.

Many of the teaching styles we've discussed in this chapter fall into the category of constructivist teaching styles. These styles put the focus on groups and are driven by the students' desire to learn. Many of the styles rely on alternative teaching techniques such as coaching, modeling, and using rubrics to prepare students for test preparation, requiring student participation to be successful. Criticism of constructivist teaching styles argues that they are geared more toward students who often dominate the class discussion, overshadowing more introverted students who prefer observation. The counterargument to this critique is that students who are more passive learners can learn through their observations.

While there are numerous teaching styles an educator can use, the development of a teacher's unique style shouldn't be cast aside in the name of student-centric learning. Teachers need to be able to pull a variety of pieces that work for them from several different models to be used to meet the needs of a diverse student population. Teaching styles aren't an all-or-nothing proposition. They exist on a spectrum, allowing the teacher to simultaneously use multiple styles or switch them up as the subject or student group changes. Don't be afraid to evaluate your teaching style and try new things. After all, your goal is to be the best possible educator for your students.

Chapter 2: Evidence-Based Teaching Tactics and Learning Methods

Ducklings learn to survive by copying their mother's behavior. Imitation is observable in many species, including humans. And we are at an advantage: we can choose deliberately what and whom to imitate. Through trial and error, we can switch between models. It is only natural that we want to mimic models and practices that are more likely to serve us well. If we wanted to become better at playing basketball, we would learn from LeBron James. If we wanted to ace business automatization and franchising, we'd seek out the teachings of Ray Kroc, the businessman purchasing the franchising rights of McDonald's and turning it into … well, McDonald's. If we wanted to become the best teachers or the fastest learners, we would need to look for role models in those fields of expertise. We could pick individuals such as Peter Tabichi, a Kenyan science teacher, who earned the honorary title of the world's best teacher in 2019.[ii] Better yet, we would search for proven systems that helped teachers, including Mr. Tabichi, become great.

Evidence-based teaching strategies and learning methods are research-backed practices. Scientists, a wide variety of teachers, students, and data analysts work hard day by day to present the world with research-backed, successful tips and techniques to educate future generations. In this chapter I will present high-quality, peer-reviewed research and meta-analyses to help you determine which teaching and learning tactics could be the most effective for you.

What Is Evidence-based Teaching?

Teachers have an impact on how their students perform in school. A good teacher who has high expectations and practices well-researched, evidence-based methods is going to have students who excel more often than teachers who don't focus on similar strategies. Evidence-based teaching methods have both reliability and validity. For a teaching strategy to be considered evidence-based, it has to meet the following criteria:

1. Be grounded in educational research as opposed to anecdotal case studies or teaching methods that have yet to be thoroughly researched.

2. Show considerable impact or statistical significance on student learning, particularly when compared to common learning strategies that may not show any impact when utilized.

3. Work for a wide range of subjects and student grade levels.

An example of an evidence-based teaching strategy is setting clear goals about what students are expected to learn for each lesson.[4] Research shows that taking the time to ensure students clearly understand what they are expected to learn leads to a 32% increase in knowledge, understanding, and ability to complete required work.[4] This is in comparison to educators who used only high expectations as a teaching strategy, which has a strong positive impact all on its own.[4] Setting explicit goals at the beginning of each lesson allows students to focus on meeting those targets.

The "I Do, We Do, You Do" Model

I do, we do, you do is a teaching strategy that includes demonstration, prompt, and practice. When we introduce new material at the beginning, as teachers, we need to deliver the content. This is the *I do* phase. As our students gain the more knowledge and skills, "the responsibility of learning shifts from teacher-directed instruction to student processing activities." In the *we do* phase of learning, we continue "to model, question, prompt and cue students; but as student move into the *you do* phases, they rely more on

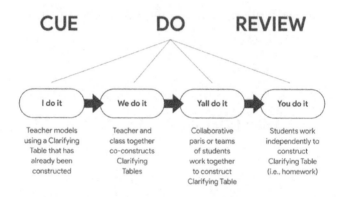

themselves and less on us to complete the learning task."[iii]

Picture 2: The *I do, we do, you do* model.[iv]

This model is based on simple principles, yet it can be utilized at all levels of education from

3rd graders to MBA students. Students have the opportunity to familiarize with the subject matter and gradually embed it into their knowledge base.

The Worked and Faded Method

MIT defines the worked and faded method as follows: "When non-experts learn new concepts, it is more effective for them to study step-by-step solutions to solved problems (worked examples) than to attempt solving problems. Worked examples are effective only when learners self-explain the solutions and when multiple, varied worked examples of the same concept are provided. Worked examples are most effective for non-experts (i.e., most of our students most of the time)."[v]

How do you do it? Present examples to students that are worked and tested. Ask them to explain themselves the solutions they got. Follow up their explanation with additional questions:

- "Why was this strategy used?

- What principle is being applied and why?"[vi]

If there are errors in a solution or reasoning, correct the mistakes and inquire with students if they see what the problem was and why. You can aid them by providing two contrasting examples. Once students are more confident with the material, fade support by challenging them to solve more steps on their own.

Teaching and learning fractions can illustrate well the worked and faded technique.

When learning fractions, students are taught to reduce their answer to the smallest unit. This principle means the fraction 6/12 will eventually become 1/2. Students in the *we do* phase practicing the worked and faded strategy will start with the 6/12 fraction. Then they will reduce it dividing it by three to get 2/4. From there, dividing by two, they will get the correct response of 1/2. As students fully grasp the lesson's concepts, they will skip the reduction steps and simply write 1/2. Reducing to the smallest unit is standard practice, and one doesn't need to write out the division to know 6 is one half of 12.

This practice leads to both greater retention and fluency in the classroom. Students are, in fact, encouraged to work in groups when practicing the worked and faded method. Research has shown this is best implemented after students have achieved mastery.[7] While this phase of the teaching model increases retention and leads to mastery of knowledge, the stage is most effective when spaced out over time. Distributed practice, when mastery is achieved over time, differs from massed practice, where students focus on the completion of the learning process in one sitting.[8]

Distributed Practice

Whether you're a student or a teacher, have you ever invested an abundance of resources to ensure you learned or taught well the curriculum essentials? Yet once you or your students took the written exam, the material mysteriously vanished from memory? Can you relate to this case?

This situation is ubiquitous. But it's easy to prevent it. If we focus on cramming as much knowledge in our heads as fast as possible (massed practice), long-term retention will suffer. This is where distributed practice comes into play. It is a tested and proven method to encourage long-lasting information retention. Students who use this high-impact learning strategy earn about 15% higher test scores and grades than students who used massed practice. One of the critical components of distributed practice includes not using a higher workload for students as time goes on. It may seem tempting to add just a little more juice to the mix as you'll be covering the same topic multiple times, but with distributed practice that should be avoided.

In comparison, teachers who use massed practice will have students complete the full learning process in one go and swiftly move on to the next topic. The same applies for autodidacts who rush through the material without properly consolidating the knowledge. I highly encourage you to embrace distributed practice.

What does distributed practice actually mean? Let's start by examining the meaning of each word.

Distributed = shared or spread out

Practice = repeating something so as to become proficient

Distributed practice requires the student to practice in multiple, shorter sessions over an extended period of time. (For instance, repeat the same material over three short sessions, two days' break in between each.) Learning sessions need to focus on the same subject.

"Effective distributed practice in education follows four steps:

1. **Initial mastery**: Students are introduced to the material and achieve a baseline understanding of the topic.

2. **Spacing**: A considerable amount of time passes after the material is first learned.

3. **Retrieval**: Students must retrieve the previously learned information from memory during a new learning session.

4. **Repetition**: The process is repeated and material is relearned over several sessions.

Essentially, the learning process looks like this:

Short-term retention → spacing → retrieval → long-term retention."[vii]

Distributed practice is popular in cognitive psychology. Its applications extend but are not limited to improving memory, physical activity, or learning to play musical instruments. In recent years this technique broke into the field of education.

Spaced-out repetition is more effective, studies prove.[viii,ix] Studying the same subject at different times aids long-term learning much more than studying all at one time, for longer. Distributed practice proves to be beneficial in the areas of learning facts, problem solving, sports, artistic ability enhancement among others. The spacing effect is a term in psychology, and it proves that spaced out, short revisions of the same topic is better than longer review in a short time frame.[x]

Check for Understanding

Another evidence-based teaching strategy is making sure you check for understanding. There are two primary ways for doing this: choosing students at random and assessing the entire class. When selecting students at random, the instructor asks a question, allows the students to think about the answer for a few moments, and then points out a student to give their response.[4] There are some fun and interactive ways to pick students via random sampling. The random online name picker is one of them. Find it at this link: https://www.classtools.net/random-name-picker/.[9] This app allows you to create a list of all the students in your class, and then you can click on the wheel to spin it. The random student is chosen by the wheel. If you prefer a less obtrusive method, the Class Dojo app also has a random student generator option that pulls from the list of students in your classroom.

When it comes to checking for understanding of your entire class, your options can be interactive and entertaining. Some methods aiming for this goal include games like asking students who agree with a particular statement to put their thumbs up, while those who disagree put their thumbs down. Several different versions can include using true-or-false cards or having students write the correct answer on a dry erase board.[4]

Remember that not all students learn the same way. Some need visual aids to see the concepts and principles you're teaching. One way you can do this and still focus on evidence-based teaching strategies is to use graphical summaries. It doesn't matter if you create them or have the students do it as part of the learning activity as long as the summary is factual. When creating graphical summaries, the focus is on showing the relationship between the different concepts or principles they've been taught and how each of them relates to one another. Graphical summaries can also take on a variety of different styles, and you may see them as flow charts, Venn diagrams, brainstorming diagrams, and even organizational charts, just to name a few.[4]

Another visual technique used by educators is concept mapping. Concept mapping is characterizing and arranging knowledge in both a visual and hierarchical manner. Concept mapping is considered to be a type of graphic organization and has three components.[10] The first part of a concept map is the concepts, which are generally indicated by being written inside a rectangle or oval. The second part of the map is the arrows, labeled and indicating the relationship between the concepts. The final piece of the concept map is the propositions, or what is also referred to as key understandings.

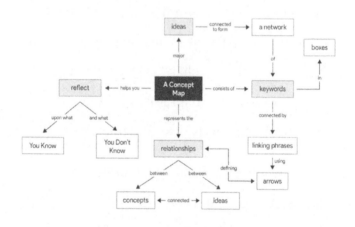

Picture 4: Example of concept map.[xi]

How to Make a Concept Map in Six Steps:[10]

1.   Determine the focus of the concept map.

2.   Identify and determine your original key concepts. This step is merely the creation of a

list of ideas. You don't need to add them to the concept map just yet. You can use personal knowledge as well as quality academic resources to make your list of concepts.

3.	Create hierarchical levels for the key concepts. There are several ways you can go about doing this. You can order the concepts in a top-down format, or you may prefer a left-to-right organization. You can also elect to color code the key concepts, with different font colors or background colors for the rectangle/ovals according to the hierarchy.

4.	Link the concepts with labeled arrows properly depicting the relationship between them. Each *Concept* $\rightarrow$ *Relationship* $\rightarrow$ *Concept* should form a proposition that is accurate and correct.

5.	Enhance your map by adding cross links and additional concepts. An example would be a concept map on dogs. You might link up that standard poodles are a type of dog breed, and it's a purebred dog that can be shown in the AKC (Americal Kennel Club) conformation ring. If you have a concept listed as Dogs and one listed as Eligible for Showing with AKC, you would indicate the concept of standard poodles with both of these with the arrow pointing toward both the Dog and AKC concepts. However, if one of the concepts is Non-shedding Breed, that arrow would be drawn back toward the standard poodle concept, as standard poodles, like miniature and toy poodles, do not shed. As you continue with your map, you might list a bichon frisé, which would fall into the same categories as the standard poodle. However, if you added a labradoodle into the concept list, the only link it would share in common with those discussed with the standard poodle would be that both animals are dogs.

6.   Make sure you proof your work for any spelling or grammar errors. Read the map slowly so you can ensure you haven't made errors. If you have a hard time proofing your own work, which is not uncommon, you may find that reading aloud is helpful. You'll recognize the errors when the document is read aloud.

Group Work

When utilizing evidence-based teaching methods, group work should be avoided until all students have some basic mastery of the topic. If students lack competence in the subject matter, they are less likely to participate, and the group work is non-productive. Or only productive for a subset of students. To set your students up for success and be part of productive group learning, all group members need to be capable of completing the assigned work.[4] Also, each group member should be given a role in the group, given responsibility for a task. The purpose behind assigning students a position is to keep them engaged in the group work and not be overshadowed by those who dominate group conversations.

Whether or not you used the massed practice or distributed practice, once students show mastery of a subject matter, organize them into groups of three and assign them each a role.[4] For example, if you're teaching sentence diagramming, assign student A to separate the subject of the sentence from the predicate. Student B will identify adjectives and adverbs and connect them below the baseline. Student C will identify prepositional phrases, which is indicated on the diagram by a slanted line under the baseline that connects to a horizontal line with the object of the preposition listed. Groups can then repeat this activity over and over again until sentence diagramming is a solid skill.

When utilizing evidence-based teaching methods, teachers don't focus on content exclusively. Those who teach learning strategies to increase understanding of content find their students perform better overall compared to teachers who only focus on content.

Additional Evidence-Based Teaching Methods to Utilize[4]

One of the best things about having numerous evidence-based strategies in our pocket is the ability to find options that work for a wide variety of students. Below, I briefly discuss four additional tips you may find useful in your learning environment.

• **Plenty of Practice:** The purpose of practice is to increase retention. While students are engaged in independent practice, teachers can check their work for understanding. If needed, they can review students' work in the *we do* phase of the *I do, we do, you do* teaching method by using guided practice. Remember, distributed practice has more impact than massed practice, so consider conducting practice sessions over multiple periods.

• **Give Students Feedback:** Feedback is one of the best tools teachers can use to let students know what areas they are performing well in, where they currently stand in lesson comprehension, and what they need to improve.

• **Remain Flexible:** Learning may take longer than you thought, so be flexible. The idea that, given enough time, every student can learn what they need to know is far from novel. We employ this concept in modern-day Montessori schools as well as many extracurricular activities where students cannot advance until they master their current level. This strategy is designed to help teachers establish the same learning goals for all students and allow students who need additional time to master the required material.

• **Nurture Metacognition:**

Metacognition is a teaching method that goes well beyond having students think about what choice they made on an assessment or what strategies they used to make a choice. To appropriately use metacognition, students would need to think about their options, what choices they made, and the results of those selections. The purpose of using metacognition is to determine if the strategy used is working and if the students want to continue using it. Or if the student should consider another strategy to be more successful.

This chapter has provided an overview of evidence-based teaching methods. Our next chapter will focus on anecdotal evidence.

Though anecdotal evidence is not backed by research, many people find it meaningful. Additionally, many students enjoy hearing these stories as they open a window into their teachers' lives, making them more relatable. Anecdotes are entertaining and can grab the whole classroom's attention.

Chapter 3: Unconventional Teaching Tactics

Sam and Pam are biology teachers in a high school. Besides instructing the regular curriculum they also spend time preparing their students to take ETS's formal AP exam. Sam gives a midterm structured in the same manner as the AP exam. As she grades the essay portions of the exams, Sam gives the students feedback on how they can improve their written responses. She reviews the multiple-choice section and explains what the correct answer is and why, teaching her students test-taking strategies for multiple-choice exams. In the lead up to the AP exam, Sam gives more mock exams, timing them, so students can get used to how much time they will have to finish each section of the test. She continuously offers feedback to students to help them improve. Prior to the real AP exam, her students have an exact baseline from their original scores at the midterm to the final mock exam.

Pam makes no special preparations for her AP biology course. Her midterm is following standard expectations, similar in style to her other courses, which are college preparatory level. She doesn't offer any mock exams, but she does have the students practice writing the essay portion of the AP exam on one occasion, approximately one month before the formal AP exam. When the students get their essays back, a score is written on the exam indicating what they would have earned if ETS had graded them. But there is no additional feedback to let students know what they needed to improve. While most of Pam's exams for her class are offered in a multiple-choice format, she does not review the tests or discuss strategies the students can use to make better choices.

Both classes arrive to the testing location to take the exam. After the administrator reads the instructions, Pam's class gets flustered because they were unaware the test was timed. As the students complete the multiple-choice section, some run out of time in the last ten minutes and bubble in any leftover response haphazardly. Both classes finish the essay portion of the exam, but Pam's class leaves the testing location less confidently. Six weeks later the students receive their scores. Eighty-five percent of the students in Sam's and forty percent of Pam's students have passed the test with an earned score of 3 or higher.

We can argue that Sam did a better job than Pam to prepare her students for the exam. Yet this story is an anecdote. The practices Sam used were evidence-based ones but the story itself is just a story. However, it ignites the fire in every caring educator's heart, "I want to be like Sam!"

Sam was intentional and consistent about her teaching method. She followed a well-working formula developed through trial and error, no doubt about that. Once she knew what worked, she applied it. Proven formulas give us, teachers, a sense of comfort without getting comfortable. But what can we do in a force majeure event when we can't rely on our best practices?

One morning a few years ago, I woke up with a nasty case of laryngitis. My throat was extremely sore and talking didn't feel like an option. I still had classes to teach, and at the university level, there is no such thing as an immediate substitute. I made a large travel cup of hot tea and set out for the day, trying to figure out exactly how I would teach my courses.

What ended up happening was one of the most exciting days I have ever had as an instructor. Instead of lecturing or talking, I got creative and wrote comments and directions on the SmartBoard between sips of tea. Because it was virtually impossible for me to write out everything I wanted to say, I had to strip my message down to its essential aspects. I also decided to break the students into small working groups and assign them a different problem to solve. After this, I involved them more by creating a code. It looked like the following:

15 Mins—Solve

10 Mins—How to Solve

5 Mins—Q&A

This was a 75-minute class. Groups were given 15 minutes to solve the problems I had given them, 10 minutes to explain to the other groups how they solved the problem. The remaining students had only 5 minutes to ask any questions. I maintained a rigid timetable as there was no additional time allotted to the class periods. The first class of the day was subdued. They followed what would be considered the traditional "group work" model. Individuals had to work with five other students, having a lead student present their response in the end.

The second class was when things began to get interesting. After I handed out the problems to each group, one student asked if groups could work together. I shrugged my shoulders and motioned back to the SmartBoard, implying if the rule wasn't on the board, the students were free to use any strategy toward problem-solving. A few of the groups did this, while others chose to work as a singular unit. Some students decided to write and display specific mathematical formulas on the SmartBoard for all their peers to use. Others treated their work more secretively. The day continued to move on as several more sessions came and went.

Interestingly, the final class devolved into a vast group session of the whole class with no time or point to presentation and questions. The students were all on the same page.

This teaching experiment, born out of necessity, turned out to be an interesting experiment of practicing the facilitator and delegator teaching styles. I was forced to simplify ideas and deliver only the essential message of the subject, allowing students to figure out the rest.

Teaching in silence was challenging and I would not recommend you play a pantomime of it. However, I would ask you to think about how teaching methods do not rely on the teacher speaking and the students listening. Both the students and I learned a lot from one another on this particular day. My students reminded me to be creative and bring some ingenuity into my lessons. And they learned some things about working collaboratively, practiced teamwork, and become more creative problem solvers.

In this chapter, we will look at unconventional teaching practices. I have tried or accidentally experimented with some of these methods, such as on the day I woke up not feeling well. Others I learned from other teachers or saw during my observations. Some of the methods we will discuss in the chapter are proven to be effective by scientific evidence, while others are not. I believe an experienced teacher's insight is valuable. I respect their ability to use unconventional methods to increase learning. We all find tips and tricks to make our jobs more useful and joyful. As long as unconventional, creative methods are producing the desired results, I support them.

Are you familiar with the Pareto principle? You may have also heard this principle referred to as the 80/20 rule. This principle states that 80% of the consequences are due to 20% of the causes.[13] In education, we can apply this by focusing on the vital needs of the students or class. By default, when we focus on those needs, students will achieve higher gains than exclusively what you teach them. Unconventional teaching methods are great at increasing gains because they are fun and innovative. Sometimes, students don't even realize they are learning. The point of unconventional teaching methods is to get both students and teachers out of their learning routines. The techniques I present in this chapter have proven to be educational and entertaining.

Teaching Tactic 1: Learning Targets

When you're working on planning lessons, you do it with learning objectives in mind. You want the students to walk away from a class or course having reached specific knowledge targets. But how often do you share those targets with your students?

When everybody in the class knows the learning objectives, it releases you from being the sole owner and deliverer of knowledge. Even something as simple as posting the learning objectives on the board each day allows students to take ownership of their education. If they get off track, you have a quick and ready reference point for them.

This practice is useful for autodidacts, as well. Summarize your daily or weekly learning goals on a Post-it. Check back every evening and assess your progress. Did you meet your daily learning target? Yes or no? Why not? What can you do differently? Such self-reflection can help you realize your learning targets were not realistic. Other times you will be amazed how many distractions pulled on your attention that day. Either way, a written summary of your learning goals gives you an anchor point that later you can tweak. This process in itself is a learning experience.

To create targets from learning objectives, create a target symbol and use "I can" statements. Your goals might look something like this:

α: I can identify igneous, metamorphic, and sedimentary rocks.

α: I can describe the characteristics of igneous, metamorphic, and sedimentary rocks.

α: I can explain how the structure of each type of rock is linked to its properties.

Learning targets are best utilized when they are stated simply. They need to require some action on the student's part, such as showing or telling me, the teacher, how they meet the learning target. If students can communicate to me they have hit the target, they should know they have hit the target as well. This makes them masters of their own education. Do you think the three learning targets above meet that criteria?

When you use learning targets, they can help you focus on what matters when answering questions and assisting students. You can even use the notes feature on your cellphone or a piece of notebook paper to write down certain phrases or trigger words to make sure you ask important questions or draw your students' attention to particular points. By creating these little "cheat sheets" for yourself, you can move dynamically throughout the learning space. You can actively participate in the learning experience without remaining tethered to a sympodium. This, of course, is more relevant in a physical classroom setting. But posing learning targets will benefit a Zoom class, as well. We will talk more about how to do it in the chapter on Zoom classes.

Teaching Tactic 2: It's Only Sensible

"Does that make sense?" I am guilty of asking this question. Asking students if a lesson or concept makes sense to them is a useless question. Students who don't understand the class are likely not going to have the confidence to admit it in front of their peers. Most students, especially those at a younger age, strive to please their teacher so much so, they will readily agree to understand what was taught, whether they are completely confused or not.

A much better alternative to this question is creating an assessment that allows students to demonstrate whether they truly understand. There is no need for this to be a monumental task or anxiety-inducing test. Students who have a history test coming up might enjoy a game of Jeopardy! while those who are prepping for a spelling test might be able to put their spelling knowledge to the test with a spelling bee between the boys and the girls; winners get bragging rights. These little assessments can be enjoyable, raise your students' level of engagement, spark some learning fun, and increase the retention of knowledge. As an added bonus, you can be vigilant for students who don't seem to understand the topic. You can talk to them after the class in private—without the prying eyes of peers that cause so much self-consciousness.

Teaching Tactic 3: Turn-and-Talk[14]

Turn-and-talk is an instructional method used to get students engaging with a partner about the lesson for a few moments. Teachers often use it to prompt students to think about and discuss a particular aspect of a lesson. However, many teachers ask themselves if turn-and-talks actually provide a meaningful connection to what is being taught. Some students choose not to engage with their partner and sit staring off into space. Other students become consumed by getting the work done and completing the task to get credit. Their partners never have the opportunity to share thoughts equally. They may focus entirely on what they want to say and talk over one another, having no idea what their partner has to share about the topic.

One strategy is to work with students to shift the focus of turn-and-talks from students focusing on themselves to concentrate on their partner instead. Help your students understand what it means to create a good and positive listening posture and body language. Explain to them the goal of the practice. It is not to dominate the conversation but to share knowledge and understand the take of the other person. Especially younger students are still in a formative developmental phase, they might not understand intuitively the importance of focusing on another person. At that age, kids are egocentric—they want to bewitch the teacher and their peers. They don't understand intuitively that they will earn more admiration and respect by opening space for others. Some kids are not taught that at home, so you may need to model the behavior for them and explain the reasoning behind it, so they can truly listen to what their partner is saying and not what they want to say. Lay out expectations of what turn-and-talks should look and sound like. Some basic rules to show respect and attention to the speaker are:

• Face your partner and give them your undivided attention.

• Listen with your whole body, give listening cues, and keep an open mind.

• Think about what your partner is saying, not what you want to say in response.

• Be respectful of groups around you. Use an indoor voice when speaking so all groups can participate in turn-and-talks.

As your students master these good manners of positive listening and speaking, you can also begin to work with them to develop more in-depth turn-and-talks. Include time for students to ask questions, give feedback, and repeat what their partner has shared as part of the learning experience. Asking each student what they learned from their partner is an excellent way to measure and assess what students learned from the lesson. These rules and guidelines can help keep your turn-and-talks organized, on task, and let you know when you need to step in with a group that isn't getting any work done. I often use Epictetus's saying when I introduce turn-and-talks and it usually impacts my students a lot: "We have two ears and one mouth so that we can listen twice as much as we speak."

Teaching Tactic 4: Predictable Unpredictability

To instantly engage your students, you can throw something unpredictable into their routine. This jolt of the unexpected perks up the attention of students who are used to working in a pattern. They may have begun working ahead, knowing without a doubt what your instructions will be. The unpredictable also works as a weapon against those who get bored easily and need something exciting to help them re-engage in their work. Let's take a look at an example of what an unpredictable lesson might be.

It is Monday, the first class of the week. Students come in with a long face, still mourning the weekend. After a few minutes of checking in, assign them a creative writing test. Ask them to write a short story about something interesting that happened to them over the weekend. Allow the students five to ten minutes to unpack their thoughts and make some headway. Just as they start to get into the nitty-gritty details, instruct them to put their pencils down. Pass their notebook one row back and two seats to the left. Ask them to read what has been written by the original author and then continue writing the story. Allow another couple minutes to complete this portion of the assignment before asking students to set their pencils down once again. This time, students pass their notebooks to the left one seat and back one row before repeating the process. After five to ten minutes, ask them to return the notebook to the original owner and for those owners to finish their stories. For homework, assign writing a one-page narrative response if they liked or disliked what happened in their story. Why or why not? What did they find challenging about trying to incorporate the voices of three authors in one story?

In this assignment, the unpredictable "passing a book around a story to various authors" works because how the story turns out is anyone's guess. We won't know until the end of the class how each of the authors alter the plot.

Note that not all students can withstand unpredictability in their day-to-day routines. Some rely on predictability, and to have that disruption in their schedule can be incredibly distressing for them. As their teacher, you already know who these students are. You can choose to let these students know ahead of time what to expect in a class so they can mentally prepare for the new learning activity. You can be mindful of their mental state during the process and let them take a brief break if the new activity is overwhelming.

Rotating copybooks probably won't cause distress to anyone. But choosing to play dodgeball to fire up some spirits can. Occasionally, I take my students out to the yard at the beginning of my class and play dodgeball for about five minutes. Motion and excitement enhances their mood and they are much more active during classes. Yet, there are some students who absolutely hate dodgeball. They fear the ball will hit them in the face, or they feel deeply ashamed if they are one of the first to leave the game. And as it often happens, these students are the target of the class. To keep the fun in the game and prevent anxiety, I tend to assign these students the role of the judge, the ball collector, or commentator. To not make these students feel awkward in any way, sometimes I assign them these auxiliary positions and sometimes I assign them to the kids who have bullying tendencies. In either case, the game is a safe space.

How can you introduce unpredictability in an online classroom setting? Exchanging copybooks via Zoom is not impossible. It is more tedious and would require some preparation on your side, but it's doable. Simply prepare a slide with pairs of students you grouped randomly in advance. Tell them to copy and paste the text they wrote to their selected partner. Repeat this process a few more times. In the end, make sure the original author of the work gets their story back. It's not as convenient as an in-person exchange of copybooks, but hey, we have to make the most of our possibilities.

Teaching Tactic 5: Short Lesson Sections

Whole-group instruction time can be challenging, especially on short teaching days if you rotate an A/B schedule: students or even the instructor can go off on tangents or ramble on when giving instructions. One of the best ways to make the most of this time is using the mini-lesson strategy.

The first step is to prepare everything you can do in advance. Complete anchor charts ahead of time to help your students instantly know the critical parts of the lesson. Post the chart in the classroom in clear view for students. This allows them to familiarize with the lesson's expected learning goals. (In the online classroom, you can set this list in the top left corner of your screen.) If you prefer to complete anchor charts with your students, consider filling in items like the learning targets, title, and prepare the chart's structure. You can cover any parts of the chart you don't want to reveal too quickly with a piece of paper. But filling in these components can help save you precious minutes during instruction time.

Another mini-lesson strategy is to try and time your lessons at home and make sure they conclude in nine minutes. While ten minutes is a nice round number and would seem to be more logical, nine minutes sounds shorter in the same way $19.99 seems less expensive than $20.00. Don't stress if you actually need ten minutes to teach your mini lesson. Nine minutes is just the goal you're aiming for and priming your students' brains. They only have to focus for nine minutes, that's doable.

Teaching Tactic 6: Hook-and-Go

While creating learning targets was the first teaching aim in this chapter, learning targets need to be student-friendly, particularly with mini lessons. This means your language has to be easy to follow, so your students are crystal clear about what you mean. By ensuring your learning targets are understandable, your students will share the responsibility of what you expect them to learn.

Invest in top-notch "hook and gos" for each lesson. A hook is a sentence, story, or prop quickly grabbing a student's interest and then sending them into the educational task for the period. The key to the hook is the length. It needs to be short, no more than about three minutes, and needs to engage your learners and relate to the go task. This strategy is based on cognitive learning theory; when students take in the new information, their brains tie it to information they already know and retain it with that older information. We use the hook to pull on the students' short-term memory. The learning task is to have the information filled in the students' long-term memory, where it is permanently retained.[15]

The last strategy to employ when it comes to mini lessons is to push students from the listening phase into the practice phase earlier. Instead of providing instruction to students who are ready to put your lesson into action, give them the ownership to do so. Try saying something along the lines of, "For those of you ready to get started, go back to your desk and begin writing out your story. If you need help, stay seated on the carpet, and I'll help you here." This will aid you in thinning out those students who feel confident enough to begin on their own. You will be free to help those who need more guidance. The best part is that it will only take a minute, rounding up your nine-minute mini lesson to only ten minutes before your students get down to business.

Teaching Tactic 7: Gamification

Have you ever become obsessed with a game or app because as you cleared a level, depending on how well you did, you earned stars or a badge? As you advanced in the game and purchased more things within the app for your character, your badge levels increased to diamond or platinum levels. Perhaps you played the same level several times to earn the highest possible badge or the greatest number of stars? Then you've experienced the hook of gamification. You understand how powerful games can be and that students can learn through play without even being aware it's happening.

As an educator, you can create games appropriate for your students' educational level. There are many options available. One of the classrooms I observed offered preferential seating. Students could challenge one another for the preferred seat by asking a relevant history question in an AP European History course. Instructors can create quizzes where students respond by texting in their responses on their cellphones. Debates, essay contests, and games similar to Jeopardy! or Wheel of Fortune are all viable options in the right classes. It doesn't have to stop there. The possibilities are endless, and students are incredibly creative when it comes to challenging their peers. Listen to their ideas and ensure you've incorporated fun and learning.

Our next chapter will look at teaching tactics in the specific subjects of reading comprehension, mathematics, and science. These are some of the core facets of education found in curricula across the United States today. Even if you are teaching in a community learning capacity, you will still likely rely on at least one of these areas as part of what you teach. Let's look into these specific tactics together.

Chapter 4: Subject-Specific Tactics

The three "Rs" of education, "reading, writing, and 'rithmetic," are still the foundation of most school programs of studies along with science, history, and technology from elementary school through college. But we often lack the ability to provide an outstanding learning experience in every subject. The closest educators are generalists who teach all subjects at the early childhood and intermediate levels up until about 6th grade. By the time school subjects hit the middle grades, teachers become specialized and certified in their subject area. This type of specialization continues into the collegiate level. Students are taught by instructors with at least a master's degree, generally as a TA, in the subject they are taking. College professors often have a doctoral degree. That level of certification implies a significant amount of time and research devoted to studying a niche area of the specific subject.

It would be fantastic if we, teachers at any level, parents, or autodidacts, could properly and adequately perform in any subject. The requirements and breadth of knowledge needed to cover all of these areas are vast. I can't promise you that after reading this chapter, you will become a polymath in every subject. But I can promise that you will learn some tactics that facilitate teaching reading comprehension, math, and science.

The Hook

Remember, a hook serves to immediately grab your students' interest. Think of your hook as a "go big or go home" activity.

Sample Hooks for Reading Comprehension

• Tell a short story related to the topic of the lesson. Make it personal. Remember, students like getting to know you.

• Share a statement about the story that isn't true. See if students catch your error.

• Ask a fun question.

Sample Hooks for Science

- Conduct a brief experiment.

- Give a relevant scientific fact. "Did you know ..."

- Brainstorm pros and cons of scientific phenomena.

Sample Hooks for Math

- Watch a video regarding the relevant principle.

- Ask a "Would you rather ..." mathematical question.

Don't forget that hook activities can be endless. There are games, scavenger hunts, and shared partner reading. Like the turn-and-talk, you can try an ask-and-switch, where students ask their partner a math or science question and then switch roles.[16]

Reading Comprehension[17]

To improve reading comprehension, the first step is to examine the titles of books and stories we read. Titles are often overlooked, as we rush to get right into the meat of the story. Take the time to teach students why the title is important. This act can help deduce the main idea of a story.

Let's say the title of a book is *My City, My Town*. Ask the students what they think the book will be about. They should be able to tell you if the story is about where they live or the features of a city or a town. When children are younger, talking about cover illustrations can be a guiding cue. You can make the task more challenging for older students by writing just the titles on the board.

Another strategy to increase comprehension includes reviewing the first and last sentences of a book or story and comparing them with the title. These sentences usually frame the main idea of the book. Ask how they compare and contrast with the title. If children are younger, you can ask them to look for matching. But as students master this learning target, direct their attention towards comparisons.

Use keywords as your students work toward increased reading comprehension. Keywords, often bolded, help them find the main idea and make excellent new vocabulary and spelling words as well. You can ask younger students to identify unknown words and see if they know or can guess what they mean. As students exhibit identifying keyword mastery, remove the bolding of these words, and ask students to independently determine what the keywords might be.

Comparing the supporting details with the book's main idea is another good way to enhance comprehension. Sometimes it can be challenging to distinguish between the main idea and the supporting content. Students can get derailed because they may mix up the two. Let's say we examine a book about a hero's journey. The story might have a legend, a compass rose, and a wanderer in it. Some students might believe that the legend igniting the action, or the compass rose guiding the hero, are the main idea. Analyzing the text together, we can point out that the main idea is a broad concept and supporting details are more specific.

Reading comprehension increases when you provide examples. Give students the main idea and three supporting details in random order. Ask them to point out which statement is the main idea and why. The goal is to help them become comfortable identifying main points regularly. You can do this with book titles and thesis statements as well.

Help students learn how to prioritize information from all they have gleaned. Help them categorize ideas as the main idea or supporting ideas. You can designate one end of your classroom for main ideas and the other for supporting ideas. When you list out the main idea, students should raise their right hand, and when you call out a supporting idea, the left hand. When they have mastered this practice, you can throw in additional categories such as "too broad" or "too many ideas," making the game even more challenging.

Finally, read aloud a paragraph from a book or project onto the board/screen. Ask the students to use all the strategies we've just gone over to develop a title based on what they heard or read. Next, reveal the book's actual title and see how close the students came. Were they in the neighborhood, or still a few towns away? Reading comprehension is a critical skill students need to master at every level. While some of these tips may be geared toward younger learners, there is no harm in improving reading comprehension skills among older students. Feel free to take similar activities and customize them for your grade level. Students who can't understand what they are reading won't succeed.

Strategies of Reading Comprehension: Basic Strategies[18]

My grandparents believed my uncle Robert was a child prodigy. Robert was undoubtedly a smart man and a bright child, but he wasn't a genius. However, my grandparents thought he might have been because he began reading at the age of three. If Robert had actually been reading, it would have been impressive. But instead, he had simply memorized the words of his favorite picture books. He knew what words belonged to what pages and could "read" the book by rote.

Robert's case illustrates that reading comprehension starts well before children actually begin reading. The earliest reading phase happens when youngsters look at pictures and understand what is happening in the illustrations. Eventually, they begin to figure out the words on the page are associated with the words being read aloud. To continue developing reading comprehension, kids need teachers and caregivers to provide modeling, practice, and feedback. Below are some basic strategies for developing reading comprehension skills.

Prior Knowledge or Previewing

When students preview texts, they can draw on knowledge they already possess. This gives them an understanding of what is happening in a story, article, or study. What they already know helps them to create a structure for new information they may read.

Predicting

Readers make predictions about what they are about to read based on what they already know. This helps them set expectations based on their prior knowledge. Predictions are guesses about what will happen in the future. Some stories, articles, and studies can be straightforward in their content. Predictions should be revised as more information is learned by reading further.

Identifying the Main Idea and Summarization

Developing these skills helps students identify what is important in the text. Summarization requires them to use their own words to describe the essence of what they read. This enhances reading comprehension.

Questioning

Teach students how to ask good questions about the text and allow them to find their own answers. One of the best ways to do this is by modeling the behavior yourself. You can stack the "whys" in this practice. Why did the rabbit take a step back when he saw the fox? Because the fox and him are old enemies, the rabbit was being cautious. Why is caution warranted when old enemies meet? Because …

Make Inferences

To successfully make inferences about the text, students have to be taught how to properly rely on their prior knowledge and pick up on clues.

Make sure to explain to your students the difference between inferring and stating the obvious. Let's say the book has a cat meowing in front of an empty feeding bowl. A student could state the obvious by saying the cat is meowing. The correct inference here would be that the cat is hungry. Using existing knowledge about why cats meow in front of empty bowls, mixed with the picture's details, makes this a possible inference.

It's also key to highlight the difference between inferring and predicting. While they are similar, they are not the same. A prediction is about imagining what will happen next based on what's already known. An inference is guessing what is happening right now. An inference, therefore, would be that the cat is meowing because she's hungry. A prediction would be that the owner will soon come to feed the hungry cat.

Inferences are subjective and can be incorrect. For instance, if a student said the cat is meowing in front of the empty bowl because she doesn't like the bowl's color, that would be incorrect because cats can't make a judgment about colors.

Before engaging in longer texts, you can help your students practice inference by playing a game with them. You state a sentence, and the quickest student to raise their hand and infer correctly will get a red dot. For example, you say, "Today I took out my raincoat and umbrella." The correct response would be, "It was raining." Or, "The little boy sat in front of his veggie plate, pouting." The right inference: "The boy doesn't like vegetables."

Visualizing

Students who practice visualizing the text or who look at illustrations while reading have been shown to have a significantly better recall than those who don't. Encourage your students to play the text in their head like a movie or television show.

Strategies of Reading Comprehension: Narrative Text[18]

Narrative texts tell a story. This section will examine strategies to help students develop their skills as readers of narrative text.

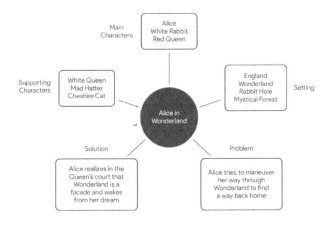

Picture 5: Sample story map.[19]

Story Maps

Story maps diagram the elements of a story. They help clarify the readers' understanding of the text. What characteristics you choose to include in your story maps will depend on the grade level and program you're teaching. Generally, they include:

a) **Setting:** When, time, place, era, etc.

b) **Characters:** Antagonist, protagonist, motivators, actions that move the plot forward.

c) **Plot:** Conflict, problems, climax, resolution.

d) **Theme:** Main idea the author wants the reader to understands.

Story maps can take many shapes and formats. The one above is simply an example.

Feel free to use one that works best for you and your students. You can always invent your own.

Retelling

When you ask students to retell a story in their own words, they have to consider what aspects of the story are most important. The "identifying the main theme" practice can come in quite handy here. You can ask your students to go a step further and develop their own thoughts about the text.

Retelling is usually a tedious task. Give students an explanation of why it is important. For example, retelling is a great way to memorize information better. Or, retelling is useful because you can double-check if you understood the text correctly. Explaining why you ask students to do something and what benefits they will get is a great way to break through resistance.

Give a structure to retell the information but also respect students' individual preferences of expression. For example, you can advise them to have a beginning, a middle, and an end in their retelling. But allow them to use their own words and expressions as long as they are accurate. Give them space to get to the correct conclusion using a method best fitting for them. Some students will draw, some will write out, and some will want to discuss the details that bring them to a solution.

Answering Comprehension Questions

Asking your students different kinds of questions means students are required to learn how to find the answers in creative ways. Perhaps the answer is in the text, or the students will have to make an inference.

Strategies of Reading Comprehension: Expository Text[18]

Expository writing is primarily used to explain facts or concepts to inform, interpret, or persuade. Expository writing is purely informational and organized with visual cues such as headings and subheadings. This book, for example, is a work of expository writing. The organizational structure of the majority of expository text takes one of the following traditional forms:

- cause and effect;

- problem and solution;

- description;

- compare and contrast; and

- a sequence of events.

When you teach students to recognize these structures, it can help them identify the association between the ideas being expressed and the intent of the text.

Main Idea and Summarization

In an expository text, we use a summary to briefly state the main idea and supporting details. It is critical that students understand the topic at hand. Comprehension is key to write a good summary. Summarizing is more than repeating the information for the sake of repetition. It improves reading skills, vocabulary skills (paraphrasing while altering grammar and verbiage), and critical thinking skills.

10 steps to summarizing well:

1. Read a short story together.

2. Ask students to underline the key ideas in the text.

3. Have a discussion about good summaries (they should be shorter than the original text, focusing only on key events, shouldn't get side-tracked into the nitty-gritty, etc.).

4. Give an example. (Use a story known to your class, different than the one you just read, and summarize it.)

5. Discuss the underlined key ideas.

6. Select five key ideas at most and focus on them.

7. Order the ideas chronologically and connect them with transition words.

8. Paraphrase the sentences.

9. Use "summary language." (Summaries should differ from the original text. This is a great time to teach your students phrases such as "according to the author.")

10. Finish the summary, teach concluding sentences.

K-W-L

Created by Donna Ogle in 1986, these graphic organizers are a three-step process used to drive classroom instruction.

1. **What I Know:** Have students make a list of what they already know about the

topic at hand in the worksheet's K column.

2. **What I Want to Know:** Have students write out a few questions they hope the text will address in the W column of the worksheet.

3. **What I Learned:** As students read the text, students should write down answers to their questions or other facts they may have learned.

After students complete the K-W-L exercise, the teacher should lead the class in a discussion of Q&A with the class.

K-W-L Chart

Title: *Stonehenge*

K	**W**	**L**
What I Know	What I want to Know	What I Learned

K — What I Know

- *Stonehenge is big.*
- *It's a monument made of stone.*
- *The stones are arranged in a circle.*
- *The stones line up with something.*
- *Some of the stones are curved.*

W — What I want to Know

- *Where is Stonehenge?*
- *Who built Stonehenge?*
- *When was Stonehenge built?*
- *Why was Stonehenge built?*
- *What do the stones line up with?*

L — What I Learned

- *Stonehenge is in southern England.*
- *Nobody is sure who built Stonehenge.*
- *Stonehenge was built thousands of years ago.*
- *Stonehenge may have been a place for healing the sick and injured or a shrine to the dead.*
- *Stonehenge lines up with the path of the sun on the longest and shortest days of the year.*

Categories of Information / Expect to Use:

- *The purpose of Stonehenge*
- *The history of Stonehenge*
- *The structure of Stonehenge*

Picture 6: Sample K-W-L worksheet.[18]

Other Graphic Organizers

Graphic organizers are a great visual tool for understanding expository text, especially for your visual learners. By showing students how written ideas can be represented graphically, it can help students remember them better. Below are several examples of other types of graphical organizers.

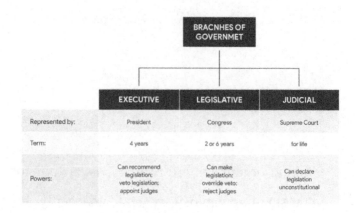

Picture 7: Sample tree organizer.[20]

	SOCCER	HOCKEY
EQUIPMENT	black and white ball goal	puck stick goal
CLOTHING	cleats shin guards jersey and shorts	helmet skates padded jersey goalie's face mask
PLAYED ON	grass field	ice rink

Picture 8: Sample compare & contrast matrix.[21]

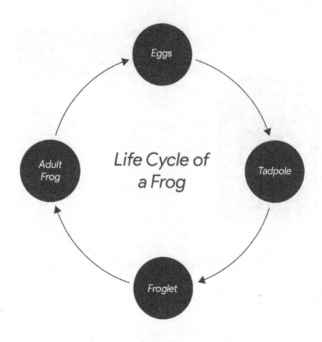

Picture 9: Sample time-driven flowchart.[18]

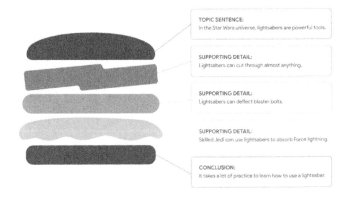

TOPIC SENTENCE:
In the Star Wars universe, lightsabers are powerful tools.

SUPPORTING DETAIL:
Lightsabers can cut through almost anything.

SUPPORTING DETAIL:
Lightsabers can deflect blaster bolts.

SUPPORTING DETAIL:
Skilled Jedi can use lightsabers to absorb Force lightning.

CONCLUSION:
It takes a lot of practice to learn how to use a lightsaber.

Picture 10: Sample steps in a process flowchart.[22]

Metacognition[23]

Succinctly put, metacognition is thinking about thinking. Using metacognition strategies increases reading comprehension because students learn to control how they analyze a text. Good reading strategies include thinking about why you're reading a given material in the first place. Is it for pleasure, knowledge, to deconstruct an argument, to bolster your own view? When you know why you're reading, you read with that intent. This includes looking up unknown words. Adjusted reading speed, for example, like increasing the pace during an exciting scene. Reviewing research results multiple times will ensure you understand how they may have a broader impact. Below, I list out additional areas where metacognition help with reading comprehension.

- **Identify where the problem is:** The fourth page is confusing.
- **Identify what the problem is:** I don't understand where the lost ducklings go at night. Where do they sleep without their mom?

- **Restate the difficult sentence or passage in your own words:** Oh, when the duck mom comes back at the end of the day, you want to know where the ducklings sleep overnight.

- **Look back through the text:** Well, if we reread the previous pages, we can see that the duck mom takes her ducklings over the hill and far away, so that must be the same place the ducklings sleep when the duck mom comes back without them.

- **Look ahead in the text for information that can help the students solve the problem:** If we skip ahead a couple pages, we can see the duck mom goes out alone, back over the hill, and faraway. She calls for her ducklings, and that night, this picture seems to show all the ducklings following her back home from over the hill.

While this example is quite simplistic in its description of a young children's book, it gives the gist of reasonable questions you might expect from a student and how you might respond. This same type of response can be modified for more sophisticated books, novels, and articles. Students may not be able to rely on illustrations. But they may choose to rely on chapter titles, flipping ahead in the book, or even making a prediction or inference to help address a problem.

The Question-Answer Relationship[23]

I am sure you always encourage your students to ask questions. Questions help the student focus on what they are meant to learn from a particular text and read with that intent in mind. If they have a set of questions they are trying to answer, students will actively read the text to find the answers. Questions also allow students to review content easier and relate that content back to what they already know.

We call this the question-answer relationship strategy, or QAR. The goal of the strategy is to teach students how to ask good questions.

Have you ever heard the expression that you won't get the right answers if you don't ask the right questions? When students answer questions, you want them to address whether the answer to their question was

- found in the text, or textually explicit;

- implied, or textually implicit;

- or the student's prior knowledge.

Below, I will use Gary Paulson's novel, *Hatchet*, about a young boy who is forced to survive a summer in the open wilderness, to demonstrate the four types of questions to ask.

1. **Questions found in the text**: What tool, given to him by his mother, does Brian use to aid in his ability to survive in the wilderness? **Answer:** A hatchet. These questions should automatically spring to the student's mind because they come up repeatedly or are common features of the text.

2. **Questions based on recall and search**: What medical emergency leads to the crash landing of 13-year-old Brian's plane in the wilderness, forcing him to survive in the wilderness? **Answer:** A heart attack. The response to these questions should be located

explicitly in the text, but students may need to look back to find the correct answer.

3. **What do you know**: How do you think Brian managed to survive the Canadian wilderness when he was all alone? What really made this possible? **Answer:** Throughout the novel, Brian comes to terms with his situation in the wilderness. He learns that thinking positively about his case has a significant impact on his ability to solve problems and find solutions versus approaching situations with a defeatist attitude. These questions ask students to draw on their prior knowledge and synthesize their understanding of the text to respond to these questions successfully.

4. **On your own**: How would you feel if your plane crashed in the Canadian wilderness? **Answer:** I would be scared if my plane crashed in the middle of the woods. I don't know if I

would be able to survive, and I would miss my family, just like Brian. These questions ask the student to draw on their prior knowledge, make inferences, or both. The text will likely not help answer these questions because you're asking the student about themselves.

Mathematics[24, 25]

One of the best ways to foster math skills is to present your students with a non-routine problem. Non-routine problems are intricate and don't have a specific strategy or approach to solving them. This means students find them both challenging and confusing. Still, if you can teach your students strategies that work for non-routine problems, they can apply these strategies to all situations when they get stuck.

This builds confidence in their math skills. Below is the four-step method to solving non-routine math problems.

1. Understand: Take the time to think about the problem and what it is asking you. Read over it several times to make sure you truly understand what is being asked. The goal is to grasp the problem in its entirety. Ask yourself questions such as:

- What information do I need to solve the problem? What information can be omitted?

- What should the answer to the problem look like?

- Are there any words that I don't know the meaning of?

- What kind of math do I need to use?

2. Plan: After you fully understand the problem, draft a plan to solve it. Will you need one mathematical technique to solve it or more than one? Types of methods you might consider include

- looking for a pattern;

- drawing a graph, chart, or table;

- solving the problem with the help of objects called manipulatives; and

- working the problem backwards.

3. Execute: Now it's time to do the math. If things don't work out, the student may need to back up to step two to adjust their plan, which is perfectly okay. Students will know they're on the right track or not by

- checking their work;

- ensuring their work is organized and that they could explain how they solved the problem to their neighbor; and

- showing the steps of their work.

4. Review: Officially check your work to ensure it is correct. This is a crucial step in math problems and just as important as solving the problem itself. Encourage students to ask these questions to know if it's time to review:

- Is this a reasonable answer?

- Are there other ways I could have solved this problem?

- If my answer isn't correct, where did I make a mistake?

Let's look at a few examples of non-routine problem solving and solve the problems together.

Exercise 1: The zoo has 15 new animals. Some of them are baboons and some of them are tigers. In total, the animals have 48 legs. How many of the new animals are baboon, and how many are tigers?

Baboons	0	1	2	3	4	5	6
Tigers	15	14	13	12	11	10	9
Legs	60	58	56	54	52	50	48

To solve this problem, we can make a table to help us see a pattern. We know that if all 15 of the animals were tigers there would be a maximum of 60 legs, but for every tiger we replace with a baboon, the leg count decreases by 2. This means there would be 6 new baboons and 9 new tigers at the zoo if there were a total of 48 legs between the new animals.

Exercise 2: Three containers have capacities of 3, 5, and 8 cups. Use the containers to pour exactly 6 cups of water into one container.

To solve this problem, fill the 8-cup container to capacity, and then pour as much as possible into the 5-cup-capacity container, leaving 3 cups of water. Fill the 3-cup container to capacity and pour it into the 8-cup-capacity container, filling it to 6 cups.

Science[26, 27]

Science is everywhere and in all things we do. Science classes are an excellent opportunity to engage students in exciting activities and build their knowledge about the world. It is one of those subjects that allow students to touch, feel, and do. This section will present segments for both younger, elementary age students, designated by the letter E, and information for older high school students, designated by the letter H. The goal is to enhance scientific learning in both groups. Hopefully, those students at the elementary level will already have a love for science by the time they hit the secondary level.

Engage Students by Asking Questions

E: Students at this age need to develop their critical thinking skills. You can help students work on this area by using the scientific method. Activities such as forming a hypothesis can help them learn to ask good questions. Don't forget to encourage scientific discovery as well by asking questions such as:

- What will happen next?
- Why do you think that happened?

Encourage students to think through the scientific process.

H: Now that the student's critical thinking skills are more developed, the goal is to keep them engaged. Ask genuine questions about the real world and how it functions. This helps students tangibly connect to science, keeps them engaged, and encourages them to ask questions. Questions you might ask include:

- Why do we care about cause and effect?
- How can technology make a difference in the environment?

Build Confidence Through Participation

E: Students in this age group can understand their world, but they do experience some level of anxiety about the future. Letting students participate and help out in experiments makes them feel more confident about science. They are generally willing to participate more readily.

H: High-quality lab experiments should be part of the science experience for students at this level. Taking ideas out of a textbook and putting them in front of the student adds a whole new dimension to learning. Lab safety is an absolute must, and students should be allowed the freedom to experiment independently.

Alleviate Boredom Through Activity

E: Students in this group will have difficulty waiting for an experiment to run. It's best to have them set up for the next experiment or work on some other activity while they wait. However, they will do a great job at collecting specimens and will probably enjoy reading supplemental material on the scientific topic of the day.

H: Dealing with a high school student with a case of scientific ennui is a real challenge. But you can be prepared to cope with this if you have a diverse range of topics and experiments. Help students stay occupied by recruiting them for setting up lab equipment and even let students choose a topic that interests them for a project. Encourage independent learning when you can. Students will find areas and issues they have an interest in or processes they enjoy.

Another approach is to consider allowing students to incorporate their own special talents into their scientific work and rewarding that talent fairly. An example would be the song "Black Death" done to the music of Gwen Stefani's "Hollaback Girl"[28] or an art student rendering scientific phenomena.

Encourage Independent Investigation

E: Younger children are naturally curious, so give them what they need to be successful. Show them safe chemical reactions, such as what happens when you introduce vinegar to baking soda. Allow students to have a kit of science supplies and make their own discoveries. It is learning what happens and seeing these discoveries firsthand that will help make your students scientists.

H: With some safety precautions, allow these students the freedom to experiment. A 13-year-old English boy became one of the youngest people to carry out cold fusion, which he did through experimentation. Make sure students have access to compound microscopes, lab supplies, and research materials.

Don't Underestimate the Value of at-Home Experimentation

You work with science every day at home. One of the main ways you do this is through cooking. For example, my wife was making a cake for our son's birthday. When she was at the store, she wasn't sure if she should purchase regular unsweetened cocoa or Dutch-processed unsweetened cocoa. After a little bit of research, she found out that "Dutch-processed" cocoa was a washing process of the cocoa bean that made the chocolate flavor milder. But because the washing took place in an alkaline solution, she had to be careful about the recipe she used. Suppose her recipe relied on the acid in regular unsweetened cocoa powder. In that case, she'd end up with a flat cake because Dutch-processed cocoa powder can have a direct impact on leavening ingredients. This is all chemistry.

We use science in our homes when we wash things, from the dishes to the laundry to ourselves. When the items we wash get oily, greasy, and dirty, we clean them with surfactants that help emulsify oils in water. Soaps are essentially potassium or sodium salts of a carboxylic acid with an aliphatic chain attached. Detergents are the same, but instead of an aliphatic chain, they have a sulfonate group attached. Micellar water, used as a beauty cleanser, uses surfactants suspended in water. All of this is home-used chemistry that you can share with and teach your students.

Adult Education[29, 30]

Adult education requires a different approach than teaching younger students. Adults have more presence than ever in education. Some are completing high school or a GED, a college degree, or going back to school to complete an advanced degree or change careers. This doesn't even account for educational settings with corporate trainers through webinars or other types of non-traditional training. Below are some tips for working with adult learners.

Keep It Relevant

You need to make the material relevant to what the student needs to know. Adults want to see how a particular skill or bit of information will improve their life in their field. They don't have a lot of patience for useless info. When preparing, consider the lesson's real-world value and relate it to the student in that way. If you can't do that, your adult students are likely to be frustrated.

Remember Your Students' Backgrounds

Adult learners have lived a little, and most of them have held jobs and may be parents. Treat them like they know a thing or two because they've experienced a thing or two. Your lesson content needs to reflect the experiences of adult learners and be congruent with their expectations.

Integrate Emotions into Your Lessons

Experienced students will often relate to lesson more if they are emotionally driven. This makes the course material relatable to adult students and increases the likelihood they will pay attention. One way to achieve this is through telling stories. These can be personal, from a student, or other anecdotes that help provide underpinning and examples for your lessons.

Encourage Exploration

Many adult learners prefer didactic teaching, a model that allows them the ability and freedom to research and explore specific topics on their own. Most adult learners do not enjoy being lectured. Instead, they prefer projects that let them solve real problems or incorporate their own personal experience.

Make Assignments Convenient

Adult learners already have a lot on their plate. Many of them work full time, have families, and all the commitments that come with those things. This doesn't mean you should make their education easy. It means your assignments shouldn't be overly burdensome.

Always Give Feedback

If students make an error on an assignment, providing timely feedback is more helpful than receiving it two weeks later when the class has moved on to a completely different topic. Adult education typically occurs at a breakneck speed. If you wait too long, you'll miss opportunities to impact the students' ability to grasp concepts and try different approaches to learning.

When it comes to adult education, it's critical to make learning enjoyable. Try to pose your lessons into a problem you want your students to solve, and then take students through the following steps:

1. **Predict:** By asking adult students to predict what will happen, they have a stake in the problem's resolution. When you ask students to make a prediction, they are challenged to think critically. They may discover weaknesses in their own prior thinking.

2. **Experience:** This step allows students to solve the problem or observe what happens as it is solved. The important part for you is to give students the room and freedom to explore during this phase. If you can, design an activity that will have students move around the

room or interact with others. Some activities include discussions, roleplaying, and demonstrations.

3. **Reflect:** Reflection is when learning is clarified and confirmed. There are many ways you can lead reflections, such as asking students to share what they've learned, to recap the lessons, or to write a brief paragraph summing up the class.

I hope this chapter has taught you some tactics to add to your repertoire in the areas of reading, math, science, and adult learners. Our last chapter will delve into the world of online learning as we look into how to make the most of teaching through Zoom and similar platforms.

Chapter 5: Teaching Tactics for Zoom Classes

Ever since the COVID-19 pandemic hit the United States, many Americans have come to rely on Zoom as a way to safely hold meetings, have school, and communicate with others. While this program is great, it has also had some rather comical and unintended consequences most users can probably relate to. A member of the UK's Parliament was giving an interview via Zoom when his ginger cat decided his master shouldn't get all the attention. The cat's fluffy tail made an up-close appearance. Then audiences worldwide were treated to John Nicholson requesting Rocco the cat to put down his tail in a hilarious fashion. Some gaffes have been entertaining or inspiring, others rather embarrassing. All things considered, Zoom has become the savior of our pandemic life in one way or another.

What is Zoom, and How Do We Set It Up?

Zoom is a video conferencing platform that allows people to meet synchronously using devices like PCs, laptops, cellphones, and tablets. For teaching purposes, you can meet with your entire class at the same time, everyone checking in from their homes. You can even record the lessons to be watched later. Both you and your students have the option of using the video feature or not, if you or your students don't have a webcam—it's not an absolute must. Zoom allows you to use many of the same learning methods you usually use in a face-to-face setting online. Some features include breakout rooms, which helps you set up small group meetings. The chat function allows people to ask questions without interrupting the speaker.

Considerations and Cautions[31]

There are things to keep in mind when using an online platform like Zoom as your learning space. This is new territory for many of us. I want to discuss some key things to pay attention to. The first thing is that if you record any of your lessons, any videos that include your students' faces are now part of the educational record and covered under the

Federal Education Right to Privacy Act or FERPA. FERPA has strict rules about how videos can be stored and shared. So, you want to ensure you follow those rules. Also, to help protect your students' privacy, have them log on to Zoom with their first name only.

Zoom is a platform that requires a list of behavior expectations, just like your classroom. It is easy for students to turn off their camera and "disappear" doing whatever they want while you are teaching classes. Some school districts have regulations that make it impossible for you to require students to turn their cameras on. You need to get creative here. Later in this chapter I will share some tips to encourage students to show up using their cameras without strictly enforcing hem. You can have the following rules to foster engagement and participation:

• Microphone muted unless you are speaking.

• Sit up and pay attention.

• Leave the teacher a note in the chat if you need to leave to use the restroom.

• No speaking over or interrupting the teacher or other classmates.

• Be dressed and have school supplies handy.

• Explain to students your expectations for exams and assessments (proctoring, closed book, no parental help).

Help students head off technical problems before your class starts. This way, they will know where to go if they have technical issues. Many schools have IT personnel online and ready to assist students with connection issues, while others ask students to email their teacher if they can't access their class for some reason. Some tips you might want to include to help students avoid issues include:

• Connecting via a wired connection instead of Wi-Fi.

• Don't run any unnecessary apps in the background.

• Make sure you've charged your computer and have the charger handy.

• Make sure your learning space is free of interruptions and distractions; no phone, etc.

Some additional precautions you may want to consider are ensuring you use a meeting ID and password for all of your class sessions. Do not post these publicly, but instead on password-protected class websites. You can also prevent unwanted visitors to your class by managing class entry to your classroom with Zoom's waiting room feature and locking students' ability to join the classroom before you grant permission. There are many other features you can use as a host, like muting talkers, preventing students from sharing their screens, and disabling the chat function to make the classroom a learning environment and not a social hour. Make sure you familiarize yourself with Zoom's many features and how to make them work to create a positive learning environment.

Tips to Make Your Classes More Engaging

Involve Your Students

One of the aspects of traditional classrooms many students miss is their involvement with other people. Due to the pandemic, students aren't communicating with many other peers. Devote a short amount of time at the beginning of the day to check in with your students. Ask them questions about themselves, your teaching material, what they did this weekend, and maybe even some upcoming plans. Try and help your students foster connections with one another over the computer. This might mean assigning group projects and partner work where students need to work collaboratively outside of the learning space.

Share Who You Are

Students love getting to know you. In a virtually unprecedented way, they have been invited into your home. Some teachers have been permitted to hold their lessons in their classrooms in some states and regions, and many have worked from home. Like the UK's John Nicholson, my pet has decided to make his screen debut to beg food or rest his head on the keyboard of my laptop to my students' delight. They enjoyed these little insights into my life. They also made comments about aspects of my home they like, and I don't mind sharing these little bits of my life with them.

Incorporate Your Teaching Style

Just because you are teaching online doesn't mean you have to teach differently. You can still be the educator you've always been or work toward becoming the educator you've always wanted to be by incorporating your teaching style. It might take more effort and planning because things require adjustment due to online formatting, but it can be done. Some science experiments are still possible, and so is utilizing the different methodologies you favor. Discipline is possible, even though it looks a little different. Let parents know what you need and look to other teachers for help if you want to achieve something but you're not sure how. Remember, you're not a lone ranger.

Hold Office Hours

Many students are getting fewer education hours than ever before this year, and parents are stressing. While many parents are doing their best to help their children, there is a national concern America's children are suffering academically. One way you can help is to make yourself available to either one-on-one or small group instruction via daily "office hours." Office hours are really more of a concept used at the higher education level, but give it a try and see if your students and their parents show up for some additional help with assignments or lessons.

Eat with Your Students

Many students have had reduced social interaction with their peers. One way you can help foster more social interaction between students and even with you is to host a lunch period with your students once a week. Everyone needs a break, especially a teacher, and maybe lunch with the teacher is an earned reward. Add a little more social time back into the education space if you can. This is something many students have dreadfully missed.

How to Get Your Students to Turn On Their Cameras[32]

Some school districts allow students to make a personal decision as to whether or not they turn on their camera for the class. This means teachers can't require students to visually engage if they choose not to. If you're in this situation, how do you persuade your students to start their video feed? Well, there are a few different strategies. You can share your own—imperfect—space as a start. If students are in their room, they might not want their peers to see their literal dirty laundry on the floor. But if you sit in your home office with a visibly messy desk, students might not feel so bad about their "natural habitat" either.

Show your students that you enjoy teaching. Teaching in the online space has been incredibly stressful, and there is constant pressure to be perfect. This is an impossible standard. If you are inadvertently communicating to your student that perfectionism is expected somehow, they may shy away from the camera. Just enjoy teaching for the sake of teaching. Don't expect yourself or your students to be perfect. We're all here in this very different environment, trying to get through it together. We are trying to support each other. Let your students know that no matter what decision they make, you will help them. While you want them to turn on their camera and you hope they'll return the favor of you sharing yourself with them, at the end of the day, you really just want them to be comfortable so they can learn.

Introduce Movement[33]

One of the easiest ways to grab your student's attention and keep ahold of it throughout the lesson is to utilize physical movement. Stand up when you teach whenever you can. You were probably already used to standing while teaching in the classroom, so this should feel like second nature. Now may be a good time to invest in a standing desk. Visualize yourself teaching in front of your regular classroom when you teach on Zoom. Classroom teachers move around a lot; from the front of the room to the back, and then they also move around as they observe students work independently. Pretend you're in that same environment. You might need to borrow an easel from your classroom. Stand back a few feet from your computer so students can observe your body language, and then do what you do best—teach!

Don't forget to let your student get involved in this action too. Let them stand and get physically involved in their own learning. Students need physical movement for both positive mental and physical health. Getting kids up and moving during learning can be fun, re-energizing, and a way to help them refocus.

Conclusion

COVID-19 isn't going to last forever, but it's impossible to know just how much this brief period in time will have impacted education in the future. It's also hard to guess some of the long-term outcomes for students. The purpose of this book is to provide an understanding of a series of teaching tactics to help you, a teacher, parent, or student, be more successful during such an unconventional time. Teachers are experiencing unparalleled stress, which is really saying something—like the need to provide dynamic, engaging lessons built for an online space with students who barely participate. They had to reinvent themselves overnight.

At the same time, parents are stressed out about many things, including their concerns about what their children may be losing out on. Students are also dealing with mental health declines due to a lack of connectivity to their peers, difficulty mastering knowledge on their own, and an insecure future. Some children have experienced a decrease in learning satisfaction because they haven't found a way to connect to it in a fun way in an online space.

By understanding how different teaching methods work with varying learning styles, teachers can actively adjust lessons to be more compatible for multiple learners in multiple environments. Additionally, by incorporating both unconventional teaching tactics and tactics meant to boost confidence and comprehension in some of your students' most challenging subjects, you foster an environment where educators work to their own strengths to positively develop young minds.

If you're in an area that is still on lockdown, consider ways with your fellow teachers to help your young students get additional social interactions during their school time. Online teachers everywhere can use some of these tips to make their synchronous or recorded lessons more dynamic. The tactics and cases I shared provide real examples you can use to encourage faster learning and knowledge retention. I hope you begin to do so soon. Your students are waiting!

Best of luck!

Gun Stevenson

References

1. https://en.wikipedia.org/wiki/Jaime_Escalante

2. https://medium.com/@joycegemcanete/the-four-educational-philosophies-part-2-230c8ee522ee

3. https://dpsible.weebly.com/classroom-management-styles.html

4. https://www.evidencebasedteaching.org.au/evidence-based-teaching-strategies/

5. https://www.evidencebasedteaching.org.au/the-i-do-we-do-you-do-model-explained/

6. https://twitter.com/andy_samm/status/1230157400570765313

7. https://www.evidencebasedteaching.org.au/evidence-based-teaching-strategies/

8. https://www.evidencebasedteaching.org.au/distributed-practice-massed-practice/

9. https://www.classtools.net/random-name-picker/

10. http://archive.wceruw.org/cl1/flag/cat/conmap/conmap7.

11. https://www.ncbi.nlm.nih.gov/pmc/articles/PMC1705977/

12. https://www.masterclass.com/articles/how-to-diagram-a-sentence

13. https://en.wikipedia.org/wiki/Pareto_principle

14. https://www.thethinkerbuilder.com/2014/08/working-together-blog-hop-with-whos-who.html

15. https://sites.google.com/site/teachingstrategiesforall/-the-hook

16. https://www.upperelementarysnapshots.com/2016/02/5-ways-to-hook-your-students-before.html

17. https://www.upperelementarysnapshots.com/2017/06/9-strategies-you-should-be-using-to.html

18. https://www.readnaturally.com/research/5-components-of-reading/comprehension

19. https://knilt.arcc.albany.edu/Unit_2:Graphic_Organizers

20. http://www.mempowered.com/study/outlines-and-graphic-organizers

21. https://sniderreadingincontentarea.weebly.com/comparecontrast-matrix.html

22. https://www.readingrockets.org/article/graphic-organizers-help-kids-writing

23. https://www.readingrockets.org/article/seven-strategies-teach-students-text-comprehension

24. https://teacherthrive.com/non-routine-problem-solving/

25. https://www.upperelementarysnapshots.com/2015/10/mathproblemsolving.html

26. https://learning-center.homesciencetools.com/article/tips-for-teaching-science-to-elementary/

27. https://learning-center.homesciencetools.com/article/tips-for-teaching-science-to-high-school/

28. https://www.youtube.com/watch?v=rZy6XilXDZQ

29. https://online.pointpark.edu/education/strategies-for-teaching-adults/

30. https://online.pointpark.edu/education/strategies-for-teaching-adults/

31. https://cdn.education.ne.gov/wp-content/uploads/2020/04/Zoom-tips-for-teachers.pdf

32. https://www.smartclassroommanageme
nt.com/2020/10/03/students-turn-on-
zoom-camera/

33. https://www.smartclassroommanageme
nt.com/2020/09/12/how-to-capture-
and-hold-your-students-attention-on-
zoom/

Endnotes

[i] https://cei.umn.edu/active-learning

[ii] https://www.cnn.com/2019/11/21/africa/kenyan-world-best-teacher

[iii] https://strategiesforspecialinterventions.weebly.com/i-do-we-do-you-do.html

[iv] https://strategiesforspecialinterventions.weebly.com/i-do-we-do-you-do.html

[v] https://openlearning.mit.edu/mit-faculty/research-based-learning-findings/worked-and-faded-examples

[vi] https://openlearning.mit.edu/mit-faculty/research-based-learning-findings/worked-and-faded-examples

[vii] https://www.prodigygame.com/main-en/blog/distributed-practice

[viii] https://www.ncbi.nlm.nih.gov/pmc/articles/PMC3399982/

[ix] http://www.yorku.ca/ncepeda/publications/KWW2015.pdf

[x] https://www.worklearning.com/2017/01/07/five-reasons-learners-experience-the-spacing-effect/

[xi] https://www.morgan.edu/information_technology/instructional_technology_-_ats/teaching_with_technology/concept_maps.html